Hi, God

Simple devotionals for a deeper life with Christ

ISBN: 978-0-359-43379-7

Printed by Lulu Press, Inc. (Lulu.com)

Available for online purchase: Lulu.com | Amazon.com | Barnes & Noble

Cover design by Cody Benjamin, created with graphics from Canva.

Back cover art and photography by: Izzy Anderson, Olivia Anderson, Gabe Baker, Gretta Baker, Solomon Baker, Asher Boyd, Kellan Boyd, Jayden Sedars, Norah Sedars, Olivia Sedars, Amanda Simon, Lucy Simon.

All Scripture quotations, unless otherwise indicated, are taken from the Holy Bible, New International Version®, NIV®. Copyright © 1973, 1978, 1984, 2011 by Biblica, Inc.™ Used by permission of Zondervan. All rights reserved worldwide. www.zondervan.com The "NIV" and "New International Version" are trademarks registered in the United States Patent and Trademark Office by Biblica, Inc.™

Published in association with Two Rivers Vineyard Church:

Two Rivers Vineyard Church
trvc.org
Mankato, Minnesota
@TRVCMankato

Hi, God

Simple devotionals for a deeper life with Christ

contents

for the Church

introduction

About two years after getting married, I was a groomsman for a friend's wedding, and in giving advice to my friend and his new wife, the officiating pastor encouraged the couple to do two things:

1.) set the culture in your home, and **2.)** don't wear masks.

Setting the culture in your home is vital, he explained, because if you don't set it, it will set itself. And as for the masks? He didn't literally mean, "You can't wear Halloween costumes," or something like that. He meant that a husband and wife are never fully intimate with each other if they mask their hurts, their dreams, their thoughts, their emotions. To demonstrate this, he had the bride and groom literally wear plastic masks and try kissing. (You don't see this at every wedding!) It didn't work very well, as you may have guessed, and on the off chance a kiss actually occurred, it just didn't look or feel right. The point was this: Truly and deeply loving someone isn't as easy, fulfilling or natural when you put up barriers.

Truth be told, both of the pastor's points also apply to our lives with God. If we fail to set the culture of our lives, the world will be happy to do it for us. And if we truly desire to connect with God, we can't do it, at least effectively or lastingly, while wearing masks.

Sometimes we wear the masks on purpose, separating real issues from our "church life" or even living vicariously through pastors and sermons rather than just approaching God ourselves. Sometimes we wear them without knowing they're there. (It's easy to walk around unaware of spaghetti sauce on your chin. It's just as easy to allow things like time and money to become "masks" in our walk with God.)

So what does all of this have to do with *this* book?

Hi, God is designed to help us set the culture – and remove the masks – from our lives with Christ. Our attempts to connect with God can often be too passive or too complicated, but here, we want to strike a healthy balance by keeping things *simple* and, at the same time, keeping things *serious*.

In the pages ahead, each devotional is designed to strip things down and let you *be* with God. We'll start with Scripture and build a conversation from there, but we'll also take plenty of opportunities to pause and reflect. Most of all, we'll aim not only to read about but to engage the Lord in our own lives. Because if there's one thing the Church needs more of, it's probably, plain and simple, *God Himself*.

D.A. Carson once said that "we do not drift into spiritual life." I don't know about you, but I've tried "drifting" into closeness with God one too many times. It's incredible (and quite sad) how often something as simple as daily quiet time has eluded me. It's sad how often I've talked about God and professed my belief in Him, only to treat Him like a nice idea rather than, you know, the *relational* God He is. It's sad how often I've woken up and gone to sleep with my phone rather than my Creator. It's sad how often I've built my schedule around strict appointments for the doctor, for the dentist, for lunch dates and for work, yet given the "most important" Person in my life nothing but rushed small talk.

Like kissing with a mask on, none of that has ever produced true intimacy. Oh, God will still nudge His own way in sometimes. But more often than not, the times I've failed to set the culture, to proactively seek out my Savior, or rather to be still and *listen* to His voice, I've missed out. Complacent faith is, at best, a weak faith and, at worst, a dead faith.

And if you're not overlooking God, you can also overcomplicate Him. He wants you to seek Him in earnest, but I've learned that He wants *me* more than He wants rigorous, religious activity. True story: I once believed that if I wasn't journaling prayers every day, I wasn't deserving of God's approval. Instead of experiencing God and then acting in response to His love, I tried to reverse the order, *acting* in order that I would properly love God and that He would be OK loving me. That's not how it works. He already loves me. He already loves you. It doesn't take a certain number of quiet times, Bible app visits or Christian playlists to "earn" your faith. It takes a genuine heart for the Lord – a heart that will happily respond to God without needing a checklist. A heart that hungers for and delights in His *presence*.

With **Hi, God**, my hope and prayer is that, as we set the culture of our hearts and rip off the masks in our collective walk with Jesus, we neither ignore nor overthink our relationships with Christ. It's why this book is *not* a sufficient replacement for the Bible, for prayer or for Christian community. There will always be more devotional books, more everyday distractions and so forth, but there will only *ever* be one Father, Son and Holy Spirit, and one Word of God. If you desire a deeper life with Jesus, you'll bask in those truths, above all. In fact, if there's one thing you take away from this introduction, I hope it's that *nothing* can deepen your relationship with Jesus better than *Him*, *His Word* and *His people*.

I may have been the one writing the words and assembling the pages that follow, but I need this truth as much as anyone. My heart is so often like a wayward frog, hopping from one sinking lily pad to another, thinking that *this* job, or *this* stage of life, or *this* new purchase, or *this* entertainment will fill me up, when in reality, it's the quietness amid the noise – the sweet, steady presence of Jesus – that touches me to the core. While I muddy it up aplenty, my life has never been on the same trajectory since choosing Jesus, and I believe, as John Piper says, that God is most glorified in me when I am most satisfied in Him.

For you, if tasting that same satisfaction in Jesus means putting this book down to spend some precious, uninterrupted moments with God, don't ignore the urge. Please do it! Because it's those moments that are always the most rewarding.

In the meantime, as **Hi, God** unfolds, let's say "hi, God," together, and invite the Lord's presence. Let's get those moments and those conversations started.

Cody Benjamin

foreword
Pastor David Welker

I can vividly recall the first time that the person of Jesus became real to me.

It was when I saw that He was more than a lifestyle, a subculture or a moral standard to live up to. It rocked my world! My life was radically changed. I saw people differently. I saw my life in a different way. And my eyes were opened to the reality of God's presence. The way that I looked at the Bible changed as well. Early in my faith, I once heard it said that the Bible is the only book where the author is always present with its reader. That always stuck with me.

That's why I'm excited about the **Hi, God** devotional. It's a devotional written in the language of relationship. Written in a way that engages the reader but also encourages every person in their own conversation with God. This book is for the person who, at times, realizes that he or she talks about God as if He's not in the room, yet longs to connect with the reality that Jesus is present. It helps remind us: He *is* in the room.

Hi, God explores themes that we find throughout the Bible, applies them to facets of today's culture and challenges both our habits and our imagination. It's written with the understanding that we worship a loving God who takes tremendous delight in revealing Himself.

For some of us, this book will be a wonderful starting point in our conversation with God. For others, it will be added encouragement as we seek to draw closer to Jesus and a life of trust and obedience. I believe that for all readers, **Hi, God** won't *just* be a pressing in to find Jesus in our journey, but more so a *response* to His grace and mercy-filled tap on the shoulder of our hearts.

I'm excited for our church to draw closer to Jesus through this devotional, which includes artwork and illustrations by the very children and youth of Two Rivers Vineyard – another representation of God's language; His colorful, creative way of getting our attention.

I'm excited for readers no matter where you call your church home. Maybe you're not yet connected to a community of faith. In any event, I believe this little book will enrich your life.

breathe

· pause · take a deep breath · recognize that God is here

SCRIPTURE

And being found in appearance as a man, (Jesus) humbled himself by becoming obedient to death – even death on a cross! **(Philippians 2:8)** ... He himself bore our sins in his body on the cross, so that we might die to sins and live for righteousness; by his wounds you have been healed. For you were like sheep going astray, but now you have returned to the Shepherd and Overseer of your souls. **(1 Peter 2:24-25)**

MESSAGE

The phrase "Jesus saves" is tattooed on my right wrist, along with a small cross. Pretty normal, right? In a culture without crucifixion, the cross is not so much an image of torture as it is the equivalent of a "Jesus fish" bumper sticker – a harmless symbol of faith. But imagine, instead, if we had tattoos and necklaces and bumper stickers of an electric chair. The cross, remember, was a horror. Physically experienced, just having arms nailed to the cross would've been like "taking a pair of pliers and squeezing and crushing" the nerve in your funny bone, Dr. Alexander Metherell says in Lee Strobel's "The Case for Christ." No wonder Christ's divine plan to die like this looked and sounded like "foolishness" to those in his day (1 Corinthians 1:18). But the physical toll was just the start. Jesus' famous cry, asking why God had forsaken him (Matthew 27:46), marked the most excruciating part of all. As R.C. Sproul says in "Saved from What?," Christ in sacrifice "became the most grotesque, most obscene mass of sin" to a Father "too holy to even look at" imperfection. He *had* to be cut off. He had to be *separated* from his Father. Being fully God, Jesus of course conquered the grave in the end, but as Sproul reminds us, it's the "greatness" of the cross's peril – the fact "that we deserve to be consumed by (God's) fury" and that "His fury ... instead consumed Jesus" – that reminds us how special our salvation is. God loves us enough that Jesus endured the darkness for us.

RESPONSE

How does the image of Jesus crying out, unable to see or reach the Father, stir your heart? **Take a quiet moment** to consider the depths of Christ's journey – into pitch-black darkness, with God's warm light nowhere to be found, all in the name of sparing you that same pain. Is God telling you something? Try listening and responding in prayer.

breathe

· pause · take a deep breath · recognize that God is here

• the perfect and necessary manhood of Jesus •

SCRIPTURE 📖

... he had to be made like his brothers, fully human in every way, in order that he might become a merciful and faithful high priest in service to God, and that he might make atonement for the sins of the people. **(Hebrews 2:17)** ... Such a high priest truly meets our need – one who is holy, blameless, pure, set apart from sinners, exalted above the heavens **(Hebrews 7:26)** ... God made him who had no sin to be sin for us, so that in him we might become the righteousness of God. **(2 Corinthians 5:21)**

MESSAGE 💬

The great story of the Bible is God literally becoming flesh and "dwelling among us" as a living man (John 1:14). But sometimes we identify Jesus only with what he did on the cross. He didn't go straight to his death when he arrived from the heavenly realms, remember? He was born a baby! He lived a life. And what he did *before* the cross – in his 100-percent human nature – is equally important. We often think of "human nature" as tainted, self-centered and sinful. But that's not what "human nature" was supposed to be. From his birth to his death and resurrection, Jesus modeled *true*, unfallen human nature – perfect obedience to God. And he *had* to. Why? Because according to his own Sermon on the Mount (Matthew 5:20, 48), God requires perfection to be in our presence. Not 95 percent goodness. Not 99 percent. One hundred percent. Perfection. So when Jesus came, he didn't just pay for our sins. He also satisfied God's demands for a perfect, righteous life. As R.C. Sproul says in "Saved from What?," Jesus taking on his back all our sins does not alone get us into Heaven; it only keeps us out of Hell, for "it is not simply innocence that gets us into the Kingdom," but righteousness. So Jesus' perfect manhood gives us the "double transfer," as Sproul calls it: We get his righteousness, he gets our sins, and we are redeemed.

RESPONSE 🙏

Jesus had to be perfect to gift us the righteousness God demands. But he also "had to be made like" us to relate to us. And he was. He was made like *you*. He knows what it's like to live in this world. He knows your struggles, your temptations, your troubles. He can truly relate. **Rest in this truth**, that Jesus knows your nature, that Jesus took care of the rest (a perfect life and sacrifice), and that he's an eternal sympathizer, always ready to listen and relate.

breathe

· pause   · take a deep breath   · recognize that God is here

SCRIPTURE

As Jesus and his disciples were on their way, he came to a village where a woman named Martha opened her home to him. She had a sister called Mary, who sat at the Lord's feet listening to what he said. But Martha was distracted by all the preparations that had to be made … "Martha, Martha," the Lord answered, "you are worried and upset about many things, but few things are needed – or indeed only one. Mary has chosen what is better, and it will not be taken away from her." **(Luke 10:38-42)** … Be still before the Lord, and wait patiently for him. **(Psalm 37:7)**

MESSAGE

In the famous story of Mary and Martha, we can easily villainize Martha when, in reality, Jesus says Mary simply chose "what is better." In other words, Martha's busyness may have come from good intentions. Still, the message is clear: The one thing that matters most is Jesus himself. Mary wasn't focused on everything going on around her. She was focused on Jesus. She was *at his feet*, *listening*. Some days, I'm a Martha, doing all kinds of "preparing" rather than simply *being* with God – like talking and reading all about how to live like Christ without actually *listening* to his instruction, pausing my schedule and opening the Bible. Most times, though, I'd argue I'm worse than Mary *and* Martha. I'm too busy to prepare *for* Jesus or be *with* Jesus. "Life" takes over, and God becomes my Genie in a bottle – a nice theological insurance plan for when *I* am finally ready for *Him*. That's not biblical. God is after us. When Jesus enters the room, only one thing is necessary: Us, at his feet. There's a surrender there. A submission. But God promises to reward it. He promises "rest for your souls" (Matthew 11:28-29). He promises a peace and a relationship that will never be taken away, either in this life or the life to come. He promises Himself.

RESPONSE

We're asked to submit ourselves and come near to God (James 4:7-8, 10). **Ask yourself:** Am I submitting myself to Him? Am I submitting my *time*? How about my *interests*? How about my *emotions*? If you sincerely desire Jesus to guide you and give you rest, schedule time – even for a few minutes – to sit at his feet. Hear his voice, in prayer or the Word, and *be* with Him. Tell him your thoughts. Tell him what's troubling you. Tell him exactly how you *feel* (upset? confused? excited?) about a specific something. And give it all over to him.

breathe

· pause   · take a deep breath   · recognize that God is here

SCRIPTURE

Let your eyes look straight ahead; fix your gaze directly before you. **(Proverbs 4:25)** ... And let us run with perseverance the race marked out for us, fixing our eyes on Jesus ... **(Hebrews 12:1-2)**

MESSAGE

When Jesus calls his disciple Peter to miraculously walk on water during a storm, it's only when Peter looks away from Jesus, turning his attention to the storm around him, that he begins to sink (Matthew 14). Is this not painfully representative of a problem we still face daily? We are told to fix our eyes on Jesus. But so often we allow our eyes to drift anywhere and everywhere but Jesus. We get distracted. In 1670, Blaise Pascal said people, deep down, crave "diversion" to hide from introspection. They become addicted to busyness to avoid confronting themselves. Three hundred and fifty years later, "diversion" remains a dilemma. In 2016, the New York Review of Books said we check our smartphones every 4.3 minutes we're awake. In the social media age, we try to fill every morsel of unused time. *Everything* is prone to interruption. *Nothing* gets sustained attention. It's why, I think, I've grown even fonder of the movie theater – one of the few places where I can and must *separate* myself from a nonstop world, *fixing my eyes* on one specific thing. As Christ followers, we are to "pay attention" to God's voice (Proverbs 4:20). That requires not being distracted. It doesn't mean we have to be robots for God, killing all our hobbies and reading the Bible 24 hours a day. But we can't expect to *know* God if we never have time for Him. Distractions are like dessert – sweet, tempting and easy to consume. Jesus is the main course – far more filling and nutritious. And when we truly fix our eyes on Him, there *is* no burden to fill time. There is a renewed commitment to being *present*, not just avoiding boredom. Most of all, there's lasting hope, joy and peace that our distractions can't offer.

RESPONSE

Set a timer for 60 seconds, then close your eyes until the time is up. Then try 180 seconds. (Or are you too busy?) Like most, you may no longer be familiar with sitting still, undistracted. **Reflect** on what may be distracting *you*. Ask God to help you stay focused. And **do something** about it. Maybe that means leaving the phone at home on a trip to the store. Or limiting TV time. Or ignoring emails until the next day. Don't be a slave to stimulation!

"Prayer is not the flare gun of the desperate or room service for the indulgent. It is the confidence of the adopted."

Sam Allberry

breathe

· pause   · take a deep breath   · recognize that God is here

SCRIPTURE

Pray continually **(1 Thessalonians 5:17)** ... Do not be anxious about anything, but in every situation, by prayer and petition, with thanksgiving, present your requests to God. And the peace of God, which transcends all understanding, will guard your hearts and your minds in Christ Jesus. **(Philippians 4:6-7)**

MESSAGE

The Bible tells us, in one translation, to "pray without ceasing." But if you're having trouble translating knowledge of prayer's importance to a *practice* of persistent prayer, here are two possible reasons why:

1.) you believe, deep down, that prayer won't make a difference
2.) you mistake proclamation for true prayer, which is intimate and relational

If we see certain prayers go "unanswered" or figure God will just do what is right anyway, we may default to the idea that prayer isn't worth our time – or if it is, only as lip service. But as C.S. Lewis writes in "How to Pray," writing off prayer only makes sense if we also believe that our *actions* aren't worth our time. In other words, why wash our hands, or ask for salt? If God wills our hands to be dirty or our food to be bland, so be it! Why bother doing anything at all? In reality, prayer is as much a vessel for God's will as what we *do*. Prayer is also not about how "spiritual" you can sound. Jesus tells us to go to our room and "close the door," spending intimate time with God (Matthew 6:5-6). That means talking to Him like the Person He is, not saying "godly" prayers just to say them. It means emptying our hearts and minds, as if to a trusted friend. "If (things) are the subject of our thoughts," Lewis writes, "they must be the subject of our prayers, whether in penitence or petition or a little of both – penitence for the excess, yet petition for the thing we desire."

RESPONSE

Be intentional with God. **Be alone** with Him. **Bring Him** with you, into your thoughts. Know He is listening.

breathe

· pause   · take a deep breath   · recognize that God is here

• it's hard work to rest •

SCRIPTURE 📖

By the seventh day, God had finished the work he had been doing; so on the seventh day he rested from all his work. Then God blessed the seventh day and made it holy, because on it he rested from all the work of creating that he had done. **(Genesis 2:2-3)** ... In peace, I will lie down and sleep, for you alone, Lord, make me dwell in safety. **(Psalm 4:8)** ... I lie down and sleep; I wake again, because the Lord sustains me. **(Psalm 3:5)**

MESSAGE 💬

A.J. Swoboda, author of "Subversive Sabbath," tells a fascinating story of soldiers from World War II and Vietnam. When WWII veterans returned home in the 1940s, happiness in the United States was through the roof. Euphoria swept the nation, as did the Baby Boom. But when Vietnam vets returned home in the 1970s, depression and drug abuse soared. Why? One theory, Swoboda explains: When the Vietnam War ended, soldiers took flights and were back in their living rooms in a matter of days. When WWII ended, soldiers got on boats and sat in the middle of the Pacific Ocean for months. Those WWII soldiers had a chance to *cry*. They had a chance to *process*. (What else do you do on a boat for that long?) They had time to *rest*. Swoboda uses the story as a metaphor for our culture, in which "we have no capacity, no time to just stop" and *be*. He suggests we've gotten to the point where only a tragedy will force us to pause our over-busy lives. How absurd does that sound in light of God Himself deciding to rest? In an accelerating world, it's *hard work* for us to rest (the irony!). Because rest is anti-productivity. It is anti-accumulation. But it is also healthy! David's Psalms about lying down to sleep paint a picture of a man willing to cover his eyes and ears from the dangers or desires of the world and simply *rest*. Why? Because God sustains Him. If Jesus can leave a crowd behind to go take a nap (Mark 4:35-41), maybe we ought to take a break, too.

RESPONSE 🙏

God calls us to faith that puts us in action. But oftentimes we embrace the action – and not necessarily God-serving action – without taking a breather. Take one evening this week to **fully and truly rest**. Cut out (or turn off) work. Relax. Enjoy God's goodness. Have a special meal. Read a book. Go outside. Watch a movie. Just *be*. If you're feeling intentional, make this a weekly thing. Why not rest in the Lord?

breathe

· pause   · take a deep breath   · recognize that God is here

SCRIPTURE

Taste and see that the Lord is good; blessed is the one who takes refuge in him. **(Psalm 34:8)** ... On one occasion, an expert in the law stood up to test Jesus. "Teacher," he asked, "what must I do to inherit eternal life?" ... He answered, "Love the Lord your God with all your heart and with all your soul and with all your mind, and love your neighbor as yourself." **(Luke 10:25, 27)** ... For where your treasure is, there your heart will be also. **(Luke 12:34)**

MESSAGE

Author Tony Reinke writes in "Competing Spectacles" that the eye candy of a media-saturated world tends to leave us bored with the Ultimate Spectacle of Jesus, his crucifixion and resurrection. The issue, Reinke argues, isn't solely the media. The cross itself, after all, is a form of technology. The true issue lies within ourselves. "Faith is a response to seeing God's glory and goodness," he writes for Desiring God. So rather than blame culture, we must first "taste and see that the Lord is good." We must renew Christ as our treasure. Right after commanding us to do just that in Luke 10:25-27, Jesus shares the Parable of the Good Samaritan (10:29-37), in which a man beaten, stripped and left for dead on the road receives help from an outcast rather than religious passersby. Reinke says it's imperative we see both ourselves and Jesus in the parable: We are the man in the dirt, "knocked out cold" by our sinful nature and the pressures of the world; Jesus is the outcast, the Ultimate Neighbor who gets dirty to save us in our most broken state. We are to come face to face with *our* helplessness and *his* outreach, our gazes turned toward the true spectacle – God's radical love for *us*. He takes pity. He extends a helping hand. He is *good*!

RESPONSE

We treasure neither God nor our neighbor by trying to do so without a foundational awe of and refuge in the Lord. We must know Him, what He's done for us and why He is worth everything. **Ask the Lord** to reignite your senses and reveal His goodness to you. Meditate on the Parable of the Samaritan. See yourself in it. See God in it, sacrificing for you. Treasure Him and His created people with continued, loving pursuit. And know that face-to-face time with both Jesus and your neighbors is far more valuable than fleeting amusements of a bored-heart culture.

breathe

· pause   · take a deep breath   · recognize that God is here

• face to face with people •

SCRIPTURE

One of the teachers of the law came ... and asked (Jesus), "Of all the commandments, which is the most important?" "The most important one," answered Jesus, "is this ... 'Love the Lord your God with all your heart and with all your soul and with all your mind and with all your strength.' The second is this: 'Love your neighbor as yourself.' There is no commandment greater than these. **(Mark 12:28-29, 31)**

MESSAGE

Just as we must rediscover Jesus as the spectacle above all spectacles in order to treasure Him as he desires (Luke 10:27), we must also rediscover our humanity – and that of our neighbors – in order to love others, as Jesus also commands. We must be face to face with *people*, too. As Tony Reinke writes for Desiring God, that often first means being *literally* face to face. "Neighboring is rooted in space and time," he says, yet we ignore our flesh and blood – we "lose a sense of our bodies" – by living distracted, digital lives with passivity. *Things*, technology included, can be tools to love others. But are we missing out on our neighbors by minimizing them? The irony of life online is that we've never been more connected to others, yet we also seem to be growing more distant. Former U.S. Surgeon General Vivek Murthy says our No. 1 epidemic isn't cancer or obesity. It's loneliness. Depression studies would tell you the same. As image-bearers, we should be leading the fight against this isolation – with embodied, face-to-face neighboring! There's logic behind it (an in-person lunch with an Internet troll would almost assuredly go differently than a debate online), but there's also *life* behind it. God's grand story is Him becoming *flesh*. We were created with *bodies*. To truly love others, we first have to *see* them for who and what they are.

RESPONSE

How do you see people? Are they intrusions to the comforts of isolation? Are they too unlikable to deserve your time? Are they just names on a screen? Or are they real, living, breathing humans, with likes and dislikes, needs and wants, and plenty of failings, like you? **Practice** being more **face to face**. With the Word and Spirit as your fuel, be the kind of neighbor that Jesus is to the wounded man in the Parable of the Samaritan – a neighbor willing to *stop* in his tracks, to lend a hand, to listen, to comfort, to acknowledge in physical presence.

breathe

· pause · take a deep breath · recognize that God is here

• loving unreasonably •

SCRIPTURE

Each of us should please our neighbors for their good, to build them up. **(Romans 15:2)** … My command is this: Love each other as I have loved you. Greater love has no one than this: to lay down one's life for one's friends. **(John 15:12-13)** … Be devoted to one another in love. Honor one another above yourselves … Share with the Lord's people who are in need. Practice hospitality … Live in harmony with one another. Do not be proud, but be willing to associate with people of low position. Do not be conceited. **(Romans 12:10, 13, 16)**

MESSAGE

At the risk of sounding like a glutton, I *love* going out to eat. When I worked for a small-town newspaper, my editors would joke that my favorite events to cover would be the ones with free food. (OK, maybe I am a glutton.) Because of this, though, it was especially notable to me when, in college, one of my friends would regularly insist on buying my meal. If I pushed back, he'd push harder: "Let me bless you!" In hindsight, I'm fairly sure that some of those times, his bank account may not have encouraged him to be buying me Pad Thai. He did it anyway. It reminds me of something Bob Goff, author of "Everybody, Always," says: "No one expects us to love them flawlessly, but we can love them fearlessly, furiously and unreasonably." Think about that. Loving someone *unreasonably*. Like, in the face of reason. Goff is no stranger to this, offering his personal phone number in his books and sharing stories of unbelievable selflessness, like the time he paid for collect calls from a state prison after an inmate accidentally dialed him. "What happens when we give away love like we're made of it?" he asks. The answer: God's love is revealed! God, after all, is the one who sets the standard. He is *unchanging* in His love for us, even though we are like kids who never learn our lessons. *That's* unreasonable love! And it's the kind of love we're called to share.

RESPONSE

There's something freeing – and contagious – about loving someone like we've got an abundance of love to give away. With Jesus as a shining example, think of a specific person and **find a way** to love them *unreasonably* this week. Get crazy with it! Love like there's no tomorrow. Do it to someone you don't know, too. Don't do it to look good, or to get something in return. Do it for *them*, as if they were Jesus himself (Matthew 25:34-40).

"We need never shout across the spaces to an absent God. He is nearer than our own soul, closer than our most secret thoughts."

A.W. Tozer

breathe

· pause   · take a deep breath   · recognize that God is here

• God is a person •

SCRIPTURE 📖

Moses said to God, "Suppose I go to the Israelites and say to them, 'The God of your fathers has sent me to you,' and they ask me, 'What is his name?' Then what shall I tell them?" God said to Moses, "I am who I am ..." **(Exodus 3:13-14)** ... Then the Lord came down ... and proclaimed his name, the Lord. And he passed in front of Moses, proclaiming, "The Lord, the Lord, the compassionate and gracious God, slow to anger, abounding in love and faithfulness, maintaining love to thousands, and forgiving wickedness, rebellion and sin. Yet he does not leave the guilty unpunished ... **(Exodus 34:5-7)**

MESSAGE 💬

In the Bible, people's names *mean* something. Abram was renamed Abraham, signifying he'd be a "father of many nations." Jacob was renamed Israel to signify his encounters with God. In fact, according to pastor John Mark Comer, ancient Hebrew had no equivalent to the phrase, "What is your name?" Because names then were not just labels. They were descriptions of a person's *nature*. In Exodus, as Comer says in his "God Has A Name" series, we get God's self-disclosure of Himself. Moses asks for God's name. And God answers with His *nature*: "I am who I am" (or "I will be who I will be," always and forever). He then lists His characteristics. Compassionate. Gracious. Patient. Loving. Faithful. Forgiving. And just. He's saying He is all of those things, and He is all of them *all the time*. The real kicker, though: Not only does God's name (nature) prove He has a personality, but it is brought to life in physical personhood through Jesus. So when Jesus says he has revealed God's name (John 17:6), it's because he has! He, Jesus, *is* God's nature. He is God's self-disclosure, personified. He answers Moses' question about what God is like. In doing so, Comer says, God makes it very clear: "He's not a force, a concept, an idea, a chapter in a theology textbook, a church, a religion, a system ... God is a *person*." He wants to know and be known.

RESPONSE 🙏

Sometimes we forget that God isn't a "faith" or a "moral standard" but rather a *person*. His self-characterization and the revelation of His nature through Jesus, a *person*, tell us He is relational. They tell us He is loving, forgiving and just. **Look to the Word**, to Jesus, to remember what God is like, to know His true name and nature.

breathe
· pause · take a deep breath · recognize that God is here

SCRIPTURE

All Scripture is God-breathed and is useful for teaching, rebuking, correcting and training in righteousness ... **(2 Timothy 3:15)** ... Jesus answered, "It is written: 'Man shall not live on bread alone, but on every word that comes from the mouth of God.'" **(Matthew 4:4)** ... "You study the Scriptures diligently because you think that in them you have eternal life. These are the very Scriptures that testify about me (Jesus), yet you refuse to come to me to have life." **(John 5:39-40)** ... Faith comes from hearing the message, and the message is heard through the word of Christ. **(Romans 10:17)**

MESSAGE

The Word is meant to dwell in us (Colossians 3:16), with "alive and active" penetration of our hearts (Hebrews 4:12). That said, the Word alone cannot fulfill, but rather point to the One who does. These truths work hand in hand. The one who "feeds on" *Jesus*, not just memorized verses, "will live" (John 6:57). Yet the Word is also a witness to him, as Christ says. So the question is: Are we letting Scripture dwell in us, and are we letting it point to Jesus? Personally, I've often tried – hard – to be a "good Christian" by relying on many things *other* than the Word. It sounds silly, right? *I'll be Christ-like without reading the only instructions he's provided!* But it happens. Matt Chandler, in his "That You May Marvel" sermon, offers the hard truth: "You will not get some lightning bolt on high that lets you walk in zeal without being rooted in the Book ... to be ignorant of the Bible is to be ignorant of Jesus." Perhaps even worse, ignoring our Bibles (or reading of it only what we like) can have us, like me, *guessing* what God is like. As Chandler says, this leads us to invent a God "too thin and too weak to be of any real value." It's no wonder we get bored with God, pastor John Mark Comer echoes, if we never use the Bible as the authority on Jesus, instead creating in our heads a "God" that ends up looking a whole lot like *us*. On the contrary, resting in the Word, depending on it as witness to Jesus as Lord, allows us to see his greatness, be in awe and know his love.

RESPONSE

God gave His Word to guide you and to know you. Pray for wisdom and seek it in earnest. See Jesus in Scripture. Hear him. And don't rely just on excerpts. **Bask in it**. Let it dwell in you. If this is how to know Christ, why skim it?

"Moralism whitens tombs, but the Gospel opens them."

Matt Smethurst

breathe

· pause · take a deep breath · recognize that God is here

• the freedom of belief •

SCRIPTURE

So they asked him, "What must we do to do the works God requires?" Jesus answered, "The work of God is this: to believe in the one he has sent." ... Then Jesus declared, "I am the bread of life. Whoever comes to me will never go hungry, and whoever believes in me will never be thirsty ... For my Father's will is that everyone who looks to the Son and believes in him shall have eternal life, and I will raise them up at the last day ... I am the living bread that came down from heaven. Whoever eats this bread will live forever. The bread is my flesh, which I will give for the life of the world." **(John 6:28-29, 35, 40, 51)**

MESSAGE

Notice the disciples here, who wanted to know what *they* needed to do to be right with God. I know I've mirrored them. Rarely is it an issue for me to acknowledge, in my head, that God is omnipotent, that Jesus is our savior, blah, blah, blah. But then all my focus goes to what *I* should and shouldn't do. I want to know the rulebook, the "10 Steps to Righteousness," when in reality, the foundation is simple: Believe. For whatever reason, we feel safe in this space of "thou shalt and thou shalt not," this idea that if I can check the boxes, I can be right with God. But Jesus flips this. He says he's checked the boxes for us. A holy lifestyle is a Spirit-led *response* to Jesus, not a way to earn his love. It's why "behavior modification" alone is *death*, as pastor Matt Chandler says: "To do the work of God is to cultivate a zeal for Jesus," not try, on your own strength, to measure up. If you try to do it yourself, as I've done many times, you end up with either habitual guilt and disappointment or arrogance and self-sufficiency. No wonder Jesus says that, humanly speaking, it's impossible to be saved (Mark 10:26-27). Good thing it's not up to us. There is freedom from "working our way" to redemption, and it comes only through the bread of life.

RESPONSE

To believe in Jesus is to believe in him not just as a healer, a miracle worker or a good teacher. It's to believe in him as Lord, as *the* bread of life. The Bible isn't about repressing our freedom. It's about giving us *true* freedom! *That* is life in Jesus. We are urged to come eat and drink what is good (Isaiah 55:1-2). **Reflect:** Are you eating and drinking what is good? Know that only Jesus, and his work, can fulfill us. Not ourselves. Not others. Just Jesus.

"If reading our Bibles and 'going deeper' doesn't lead us to forgiving others, befriending 'sinners,' giving money away, loving Jesus, serving when no one's looking, a heart for the lost ... we're not becoming a disciple. We're becoming a Pharisee. Further from Jesus, not closer."

Adam Weber

breathe

· pause   · take a deep breath   · recognize that God is here

• **the keys to growth** •

SCRIPTURE

Therefore, brothers and sisters, since we have confidence to enter the Most Holy Place by the blood of Jesus, by a new and living way opened for us through the curtain, that is, his body, and since we have a great priest over the house of God, let us draw near to God with a sincere heart and with the full assurance that faith brings, having our hearts sprinkled to cleanse us from a guilty conscience and having our bodies washed with pure water. Let us hold unswervingly to the hope we profess, for he who promised is faithful. And let us consider how we may spur one another on toward love and good deeds, not giving up meeting together, as some are in the habit of doing, but encouraging one another … **(Hebrews 10:19-24)**

MESSAGE

There's a reason Jesus tells his disciples that those who draw near to him will never go hungry (John 6). He didn't come just to reunite us with God in Heaven. He came to sustain us here and now. It's why we're urged to draw near to him. But *how* do we do that? We get a pretty clear picture in Hebrews: Through the Word, through a personal relationship and through community. Word. Relationship. Community. It's a simple formula, really, and it makes sense. The Word gives us hope and assurance and conviction. Relationship gives us personal, prayerful intimacy with God. Community gives us a chance to put love and faith in action. If ever you're feeling distant from God, sometimes it's as simple as asking yourself: Am I in the Word? Am I spending my own time with the Lord? Am I seeking community? For me, hanging with other believers is usually pretty easy. It's fun. But if I do that and then forgo prayer, Scripture and alone time with God, I'm essentially trying to draw near to God *only* through people. It just doesn't work to the fullest. On the flip side, if you're all, "My faith is just about me and Jesus!" and never allow your life with Christ to go beyond your bedroom Bible, well, that's not great, either. We're called to more.

RESPONSE

Really, all of this points to something even bigger: A life fully surrendered to God. Faith shouldn't be limited to *just* personal Bible time, or *just* hanging out with church friends, or *just* anything. Our walk with Jesus should be a walk with him into *everything*. But it doesn't hurt to start small: Do you have enough Word? Relationship? Community?

breathe

· pause · take a deep breath · recognize that God is here

• God is a Father •

SCRIPTURE 📖

See what great love the Father has lavished on us, that we should be called children of God! **(1 John 3:1)** … Every good and perfect gift is from above, coming down from the Father of the heavenly lights, who does not change like shifting shadows. **(James 1:17)** … If you, though you're evil, know how to give good gifts to your children, how much more will your Father in heaven give good gifts to those who ask him! **(Matthew 7:11)**

MESSAGE 💬

It didn't take much time as a new dad to see some of God's character in parenthood. At almost five months old, our son's main form of communication is crying. (The joy of children!) But there's this weird thing that happens when he and I lock eyes and his mouth shoots wide open with a smile: I don't really care that he's being a whiny baby (literally). I don't care that he can't *do* anything for me. If anything, in fact, all he does is *take* from me and his mom – time, attention, money. Yet when he sees me and I see him, and he gives his dad a cheesy moment of affection, that makes it all worth it. He's my little man. And I love him! Is that not a picture of how God sees us? We don't do nearly enough for Him. We take from Him. We can be some pretty whiny babies, too. And yet, through Jesus, we see that God is a loving Father, cherishing us *at all times*. The most astounding thing is that He doesn't stop there. Consider this: If my son is still being a whiny baby in 30 years, there would have to be some serious consequences for him. I'd *have* to punish him, right? God is different. Thirty years could pass, I could be struggling with the same things, perhaps wanting to punish *myself*, and yet *He* will never *want* to punish me. It's ridiculous! But that's God's love! As pastor Matt Chandler says, we are far more surprised at our failures than God is. Following Him is like being a kid to the world's best parent. As Chandler says, it is "willing to be confronted a million times between here and glory and have Him expose in you what you thought was no longer in you over and over again, and be met by grace, met by steadfast love, met by kindness over and over again." *That* is one amazing Father.

RESPONSE 🙏

How have your experiences of family, whether as someone's children or parents, shown glimpses of – and/or fallen short of – God's fatherhood? How do you, personally, recognize God as a Father? **Reflect** on His character.

breathe

· pause · take a deep breath · recognize that God is here

SCRIPTURE

But the fruit of the Spirit is love, joy, peace, forbearance, kindness, goodness, faithfulness, gentleness and self-control ... Those who belong to Christ Jesus have crucified the flesh with its passions and desires. Since we live by the Spirit, let us keep in step with the Spirit. **(Galatians 5:22-25)** ... Better a patient person than a warrior, one with self-control than one who takes a city. **(Proverbs 16:32)**

MESSAGE

If you've ever watched "Star Wars," you've probably heard of "hyperspace," which is essentially a dimension in which spaceships can move faster than the speed of light. It's used to get to way more places – and accomplish way more things – in way less time. Isn't it a perfect metaphor for our culture? We live like we're in hyperspace. Whether it's on our smartphones or on our calendars, we seem to have an increasing obsession with doing things and doing them *fast* so as not to miss out on doing more things. It's go, go, go, go, go, and if you have to take a break, make sure you're doing something while you break! In response to feeling like we have less marginal time, author Tony Reinke writes, we just accelerate faster – we download more apps to "save time" with other tasks, we listen to podcasts sped up, we scan everything we read. Not only does this minimize everything into smaller chunks, blurring the lines between serious and shallow interests (my "Jesus time" and "Instagram time" both get 1/278th of my day, hooray!), but it also runs counter to the Bible's teaching on spiritual growth. How often are we told that cultivating and sharing faith in Jesus is about sowing seeds and reaping a harvest? That's a patient process! Imagine if Jesus operated on hyperspeed in Luke 8:40-48, when he stopped right in the middle of a huge crowd anxious for his miracles in order to heal a woman desperate for his touch. He should be our model not only for everyday life but for how we seek him – with a patience and restraint that *allows* us freedom to do what's best.

RESPONSE

Constantly cramming more into less time isn't so much "self-control" as it is slavery to productivity. To bear the fruit of the Spirit includes making sure we don't suffocate it. In what ways must you slow down? How can you keep in step with the Spirit? It may mean cutting certain things off, or limiting them. Pray for renewed focus.

breathe

· pause · take a deep breath · recognize that God is here

SCRIPTURE

Lord, our Lord, how majestic is your name in all the earth! ... When I consider your heavens, the work of your fingers, the moon and the stars, which you have set in place, what is mankind that you are mindful of them, human beings that you care for them? **(Psalm 8:1, 3-4)** ... The Lord wraps himself in light as with a garment; he stretches out the heavens like a tent and lays the beams of his upper chambers on their waters ... How many are your works, Lord! In wisdom you made them all; the earth is full of your creatures ... All creatures look to you to give them their food at the proper time ... when you open your hand, they are satisfied with good things ... May the glory of the Lord endure forever; may the Lord rejoice in his works – he who looks at the earth, and it trembles, who touches the mountains, and they smoke. **(Psalm 104:2-3, 24, 27-28, 31-32)**

MESSAGE

When's the last time you looked at the stars? Like, *really* looked? If you sit outside during a cool night, surrounded by the scents of summer grass, the sounds of chirping crickets and the sights of an endless sky, staring upward as if to see how far your gaze can go, I'm not sure it's possible to *not* be in awe. It can't be a coincidence that God's *divine* nature is revealed through His *created* nature (Romans 1:20). There is so much to learn about the Lord through the creation around us: His radiant light, seen in the sun; His unthinkable depth; evoked through the stars and oceans; His enduring patience, modeled by the stillness of trees. But do we take time to realize it? Alan Noble, author of "Disruptive Witness," says we invite God's presence when we acknowledge the transcendent. That means *seeing* His majesty in everything around us! In a manufactured world, where even our Sunday morning journey to church is buoyed by human innovation (alarm clock! processed breakfast food! self-routing car! radio music!), this can be a challenge. But how amazing it is when we notice the supernatural by engaging the *natural*. David's Psalms here are full of physical imagery, urging us to find hints of God in the tangible things right outside your door.

RESPONSE

Find a quiet place or moment in nature – a visit to a park, or even a couple minutes on the doorstep – and **look**. Pause everything else and *consider* creation. Listen to the birds. Scan the horizon. Marvel at the Lord!

"Following your heart is the problem, not the solution."

Matt Smethurst

breathe

· pause · take a deep breath · recognize that God is here

SCRIPTURE 📖

Indeed, there is no one on earth who is righteous, no one who does what is right and never sins. **(Ecclesiastes 7:20)** … The Lord looks down from heaven on all mankind to see if there are any who understand, any who seek God. All have turned away, all have become corrupt; there is no one who does good, not even one. **(Psalm 14:2-3)** … But God demonstrates his own love for us in this: While we were still sinners, Christ died for us. Since we have now been justified by his blood, how much more shall we be saved from God's wrath through him! For if, while we were God's enemies, we were reconciled to him through the death of his Son, how much more, having been reconciled, shall we be saved through his life! **(Romans 5:8-10)**

MESSAGE 💬

Whether it's songs or movies or just the mouths of the celebrities who make them, pop culture is often a megaphone through which popular beliefs are preached. It shouldn't be too surprising, then, that in America, where individualism has long reigned as the supreme "dream," our arts have reflected a self-made mentality. Among the hit mottos: "Be true to yourself" and "Do what makes *you* happy." Now, it's not wrong to want to better yourself or understand your worth. Humans have made other humans feel pretty worthless at many points in history. But as an ultimate way to life, being yourself just won't cut it. Chris Pratt, of "Avengers" and "Guardians of the Galaxy" fame, surely stirred some in Hollywood at the 2018 MTV Movie & TV Awards by declaring exactly that: "People are going to tell you're perfect just the way you are. You're not! You are *imperfect*. You always will be." Deep down, we should all agree – we are not flawless. But the Gospel doesn't end it there, Pratt added. It doesn't leave us in brokenness. Instead, it offers Jesus as God's blood-bought gift of grace. It's why, as pastor Tim Keller says on the "Signposts" podcast, we become Christians when we repent not only of doing bad things but of being self-savers and self-justifiers. We *can't* be our own saviors. Thanks to Jesus, we don't have to be.

RESPONSE 🙏

We may scoff at society's me-first approach, but if we claim Jesus as Lord and savior yet put all our trust in ourselves, are we any better? Who do you rely on? Be honest with yourself, and remember God's grace!

"Prosperity theology: Step over Christ's cross to pick up world's crown.
Biblical theology: Step over world's crown to pick up Christ's cross."

Matt Smethurst

breathe

· pause   · take a deep breath   · recognize that God is here

SCRIPTURE ⬜

Then he (Jesus) said to them, "Watch out! Be on your guard against all kinds of greed; life does not consist in an abundance of possessions." **(Luke 12:15)** ... As goods increase, so do those who consume them. And what benefit are they to the owners except to feast their eyes on them? **(Ecclesiastes 5:11)** ... "Do not store up for yourselves treasures on earth, where moths and vermin destroy, and where thieves break in and steal. But store up for yourselves treasures in heaven, where moth and vermin do not destroy, and where thieves do not break in and steal." **(Matthew 6:19-21)** ... Keep your lives free from the love of money and be content with what you have, because God has said, "Never will I leave you; never will I forsake you." **(Hebrews 13:5)**

MESSAGE 💬

You know that classic Dunkin' Donuts slogan, "America runs on Dunkin'?" Research would indicate the United States deserves a different phrase: "America runs on shoppin'." MarketWatch said in 2017 that most U.S. income goes toward luxuries, not necessities. We also buy more than we can afford. As Trevin Wax writes in "This Is Our Time," even our entire holiday calendar is monetized – from Christmas to Valentine's Day, there's *always* an excuse to be purchasing something. The problem isn't just money. It's this constant wanting, needing and accumulating *more*. Consumerism. The side effects can be deadly, from work becoming your religion to "ungrateful" becoming your mood of choice. Perhaps most deceiving of all, it can transform Jesus from a necessity to a luxury. In a culture of consumerism, success is defined by moving from poverty to wealth (or wealth to *more* wealth). *I haven't made it until I get a car, then a house, then a ...* And while following Jesus certainly *has* its benefits, Christ didn't ask to be one of many therapeutic options for our life of personal accumulation. He didn't ask to be an add-on. He asked to be *everything*. Wax urges us to replace the question, "Am I keeping up with the Joneses?" with another question: "Am I looking more like Jesus?"

RESPONSE 🙏

Have you ever felt the weight of consumerism? More stuff leading to a desire for more stuff? Or Jesus looking less like Lord and more like an ego booster? Is there a particular area of your life, your expenses, your consumption that needs adjusting? God has grace for you. But He calls us to cling to Him above all.

breathe

• pause   • take a deep breath   • recognize that God is here

SCRIPTURE

"Not everyone who says to me, 'Lord, Lord,' will enter the kingdom of heaven, but only the one who does the will of my Father who is in heaven. Many will say to me on that day, 'Lord, Lord, did we not prophesy in your name and in your name drive out demons and in your name perform many miracles?' Then I will tell them plainly, 'I never knew you. Away from me, you evildoers!'" **(Matthew 7:21-21)** … "The work of God is this: to believe in the one he has sent." **(John 6:29)** … For God so loved the world that he gave his one and only Son, that whoever believes in him shall not perish but have eternal life. For God did not send his Son into the world to condemn the world, but to save the world through him. Whoever believes in him is not condemned, but whoever does not believe stands condemned already because they have not believed in the name of God's one and only Son. **(John 3:16-18)**

MESSAGE

I'm not sure there's a verse that's fascinated (or scared) me more than in Matthew 7, when Jesus says, "I never knew you." Like, you can be a miracle worker, a literal demon slayer – a spiritual superhero! But unless you *know* Jesus, none of your heroics ultimately matter. If he doesn't *know* you, he'll turn away from you. That's intense! So how *do* we truly know him? Maybe the first step is asking another question: How would we get to know anyone else? In order to *know* my wife and not just know *about* her, I had conversations with her, I interacted with her, and I ultimately sacrificed for her – time, energy, attention. Unlike, say, Abraham Lincoln, who plenty of people know *about*, I *know* my wife on a personal level. That's mostly because I believed she was worth knowing, and that she *could* be known. Jesus is clearly suggesting he *can* be known. If we believe in him as the one God sent to save us, as *Lord* of our *lives*, then knowing him like anyone else – with personal time, talks and trust – should follow.

RESPONSE

Do you feel as if you *know* Jesus or know *about* him? If it's the latter, consider how much deeper, how much more powerful, it would be to *personally* interact with your Creator and Savior. That's God's heart for His people. To call us His children (1 John 3:1), to be a loved one we know and trust and believe in. **Consider:** Is there something you could do – or sacrifice – to know Jesus better? His companionship is worth it.

"In Christmas, we see God making the first move. He always has. From chasing mankind in the Garden to His 'come now' moment in Isaiah 1 to the birth, death and resurrection of Jesus … it's all God making the first move. Our faith is by His invitation."

David Welker

breathe

· pause   · take a deep breath   · recognize that God is here

SCRIPTURE 📖

"No one can come to me unless the Father who sent me draws them … " **(John 6:44)** … "When (the Holy Spirit) comes, he will prove the world to be in the wrong about sin and righteousness and judgment … " **(John 16:8)** … "But when he, the Spirit of truth, comes, he will guide you into all the truth." **(John 16:13)**

MESSAGE 💬

Do we find God, or does God find us? It's a deep and layered question, but I think it has value when it comes to our day-to-day perspective of Jesus. I know I've often made my faith about me. I've heard plenty of stories about people "finding Jesus," including my own, that end up painting the people – and not Jesus – as the hero. Truth be told, the Bible tells us that *no one* seeks God on their own (Romans 3:10-12). We're too broken to do that. Jesus himself seems to reiterate this in John 6, repeatedly assuring disciples that "no one" comes to him unless they've been drawn by God. Thankfully, Jesus also seems to clarify where the "drawing" comes from in John 16: A personal Spirit will convict us of our shortcomings and showcase the truth of Jesus. We, of course, are called to respond with belief (not a perfect life, or a thousand good deeds; just belief!). But first comes God's spurring surge of grace. *He* reaches out to *us*. As 18th-century theologian John Gill says, we aren't drawn by God to Jesus through some kind of "moral persuasion," but rather by the "powerful influence" of His love and grace. It is "an act of power, yet not of force," Gill says, not unlike the way romance *draws* the heart and music *draws* the ears. Mika Edmondson writes in "The New City Catechism" that this proves our redemption is entirely a result of divine compassion. It's not *us* making the most of salvation offered to us. It's God, in Christ and the Spirit, showing us how awesome *He* is. "In and of ourselves," Edmondson writes, "we are no better than our non-Christian neighbors. The only difference is that something (or, rather, someone) absolutely wonderful has come into our lives and changed everything."

RESPONSE 🙏

If you call yourself a follower of Jesus, you probably, at one point or another, made a conscious decision to follow him. The same goes for knowing him – you make conscious decisions to spend time with him, to know him better. **Remember**, however, that *He* drew *you*, that He *still* draws you, and your hunger for Him will grow all the more!

breathe

· pause · take a deep breath · recognize that God is here

• the Spirit is a witness •

SCRIPTURE

... if Christ is in you, then even though your body is subject to death because of sin, the Spirit gives life because of righteousness ... For those who are led by the Spirit of God are the children of God. The Spirit you received does not make you slaves, so that you live in fear again; rather, the Spirit you received brought about your adoption to sonship. And by him we cry, 'Abba, Father.' The Spirit himself testifies with our spirit that we are God's children ... the Spirit helps us in our weakness. We do not know what we ought to pray for, but the Spirit himself intercedes for us through wordless groans. **(Romans 8:10, 14-16, 26)** ... The world cannot accept him, because it neither sees him nor knows him. But you know him, for he lives with you and will be in you. **(John 14:17)**

MESSAGE

If we could have our choice between the Holy Spirit within us or Jesus right beside us, which would we choose? The astounding thing about Jesus leaving the world and ascending to Heaven after being resurrected is that he assures his disciples that it is "for your good that I am going away" (John 16:7). For your *good*! Some translations have him saying it is "better" that he leaves than stays. Crazy, right? It sounds illogical to any of us who think we'd be better followers of Jesus if he were still here, but that's only if we ignore his corresponding promise of the Holy Spirit's presence. Not only is the Spirit our guide to lives that better resemble Christ (Galatians 5:22-23) and a testimony about Jesus (John 16:14-15), but the Spirit bears witness about our position as sons and daughters of God. As pastor Matt Chandler says, he "does the work of illumination," reminding us, always, that we are God's children. He lives with us and in us, a relational being like the Father and Son, and he's here to help us every step of the way.

RESPONSE

"If you have a desire to follow Jesus," Chandler says, "a desire to submit all the more to his lordship, *regardless of how well you're doing that*, that's the Spirit, testifying that you're children of God." Do you sense that testimony in yourself? Have you felt the Spirit's groans on your behalf? Those urges to get your eyes back on Jesus during the struggles or distractions of life? Let the Spirit's presence assure you of your security as God's own. **Invite him in**, here and now. **Hear his urges**, even if they're subtle. Ask him to guide you, and **move** in his peace and power.

69

"In a nutshell, the Bible from Genesis 3 to Revelation 22 tells the story of a God reckless with desire to get his family back."

Philip Yancey

breathe

· pause · take a deep breath · recognize that God is here

• Jesus steals us back •

SCRIPTURE

"Or again, how can anyone enter a strong man's house and carry off his possessions unless he first ties up the strong man? Then he can plunder his house." **(Matthew 12:29)** … Can plunder be taken from warriors, or captives be rescued from the fierce? But this is what the Lord says: "Yes, captives will be taken from warriors, and plunder retrieved from the fierce; I will contend with those who contend with you, and your children I will save." **(Isaiah 49:24-25)** … The one who does what is sinful is of the devil, because the devil has been sinning from the beginning. The reason the Son of God appeared was to destroy the devil's work. **(1 John 3:8)**

MESSAGE

Jesus' words about tying up a strong man come immediately after religious leaders accuse him of using demonic power to cast out … demons. Silly accusation, right? Why would a demon cast out his own kind? Jesus himself says something similar: "If Satan drives out Satan, he is divided against himself" (Matthew 12:26). But the strong-man story isn't just a way of Jesus driving home the point that he is not demonic, but rather an *enemy* of the demonic. It also paints a picture of Jesus' impact on *our* lives, today. As Bridgetown Church's Josh Porter notes, if the strong man in the story is Satan, then Jesus is the rebel who enters Satan's dominion. And "what Jesus is stealing from the Devil," Porter says, "is us." Did Jesus come to forgive sins and bridge the gap between us and God? Absolutely. But first he had to "tie up" the Devil. Being the imperfect people that we are, we belong to the death and destruction of our enemy until Christ recaptures us (Hebrews 2:14). It's why the Bible tells us that Jesus' mission "was to destroy the devil's work" (1 John 3:8). That's what his life was about: Stealing us back to set us free.

RESPONSE

Sometimes, in Christian circles, we like to associate wrath and power with God, the Old Testament Father, and then associate love and forgiveness with Jesus, the New Testament Son. It's as if we view them as two different gods with two different personalities, when in reality, Jesus says they are "one" (John 10:30). In the strong-man stories of Matthew and Isaiah, we see not only Jesus' love for us but the power that accompanies it. What feelings or thoughts come to mind knowing Jesus came to steal *you* back? How can you **respond** to his actions today?

73

breathe

· pause · take a deep breath · recognize that God is here

SCRIPTURE

"Therefore I tell you, do not worry about your life, what you will eat or drink; or about your body, what you will wear. Is not life more than food, and the body more than clothes? Look at the birds of the air; they do not sow or reap or store away in barns, and yet your heavenly Father feeds them. Are you not much more valuable than they? Can any one of you by worrying add a single hour to your life?" **(Matthew 6:25-27)** ... The Lord is my strength and my shield; my heart trusts in him, and he helps me. **(Psalm 28:7)** ... For the Spirit God gave us does not make us timid, but gives us power, love and self-discipline. **(2 Timothy 1:7)**

MESSAGE

I once met a man named Prince. Believe it or not, his name wasn't the most unique thing about him. What really stood out was how consistently *unafraid* he was. In fact, I'm not sure I've ever encountered someone so sure of God's presence. As Christians, of course, we shouldn't be ashamed if we encounter doubts. The Gospel Coalition wisely notes that doubt "is often the birth pangs of deepened faith." But my friend Prince modeled something we're all afforded as followers of Jesus: Authority. By that, I don't mean arrogant dominion. I mean *power* over the worries of the life in front of you – a power rooted in God's peace, provisions and promises. Prince was convinced that if he didn't live with authority over circumstances, then circumstances would have authority over him. He reminded me that, many times, we can *choose* peace, not because *we're* strong-willed but because *God* is with us. That's Matthew 6:25-34 in action! And really, it's just trust in the Lord. It's a living belief that circumstances ultimately have no power over the goodness of our Father, our closeness with Him or His plans for our life.

RESPONSE

To have peace – to walk in authority – isn't necessarily to have no fears. It's to recognize those fears and declare, "God is greater." Is exercising this kind of authority difficult for you personally? Are there particular areas of your life that are easier to have authority over? Are you walking with authority over your circumstances – trusting in God to provide exactly what you need? **Reflect** on your own experiences, then ask the Lord to grant you more peace, whether it's in standing out from the crowd, loving Him more abundantly or conquering life's obstacles.

"Christianity in America ... has been ravaged by the dominant idea that a decision *for* God is more defining than delight *in* God."

John Piper

breathe

· pause   · take a deep breath   · recognize that God is here

SCRIPTURE 📖

What good is it, my brothers and sisters, if someone claims to have faith but has no deeds? Can such faith save them? Suppose a brother or a sister is without clothes and daily food. If one of you says to them, "Go in peace; keep warm and well fed," but does nothing about their physical needs, what good is it? In the same way, faith by itself, if it is not accompanied by action, is dead ... You believe that there is one God. Good! Even the demons believe that – and shudder ... You see that a person is considered righteous by what they do and not by faith alone ... As the body without the spirit is dead, so faith without deeds is dead. **(James 2:14-17, 19, 24, 26)** ... "Why do you call me, 'Lord, Lord,' and do not do what I say?" **(Luke 6:46)**

MESSAGE 💬

God is insanely and incredibly paradoxical, isn't He? On one hand, an omnipresent creator of life; on another, a baby born in a manger. A king of kings, yet a servant of servants. The list goes on. And it extends to His view of us. On one hand, God wants *all* to be saved, gave himself as a ransom for *all* (1 Timothy 2:4-6) and frees us through *His* grace/Son/sacrifice alone (Romans 3:23-24). That means you can be as evil as Hitler or as good as Gandhi, but it's still *only* Jesus who can swap his righteousness for your sin, freely redeeming you and freeing you from trying to do so by your own efforts. And yet, despite all that, Jesus suggests over and over again that this grace should – or must – warrant a *response*. To say, "Jesus is Lord," is not enough. Because Jesus isn't asking followers to pray a prayer of salvation, then go about their merry lives. He's asking for repentance (Mark 1:15), which means an active *turn* from sinful ways. He's asking us to *count the cost* of following him, much like we'd count the cost of a war or a construction project before actually giving them the green light (Luke 14:25-33). He's telling us, cut and dry, that if we do not give up *everything*, we *cannot* be his disciples. The unconditional love is still there. Jesus came to *save*, not condemn (John 3:16). But the surest sign of true belief in that saving grace, as James says, is a responsive life.

RESPONSE 🙏

If a homeless, hated Jesus were here, asking you to give everything up to follow him, would you? We're not called to be perfect, but we are called to put faith in action. Feel God's love, but count His cost. Know He didn't ask just for a prayer, but for *life* in Christ For surrender. For repentance. And **know** He is worth it!

breathe

· pause   · take a deep breath   · recognize that God is here

• **radical reality** •

SCRIPTURE

"Enter through the narrow gate. For wide is the gate and broad is the road that leads to destruction, and many enter through it. But small is the gate and narrow the road that leads to life, and only a few find it." **(Matthew 7:13-14)** … "Some people are like seed along the path, where the word is sown. As soon as they hear it, Satan comes and takes away the word that was sown in them. Others, like seed sown on rocky places, hear the word and at once receive it with joy. But since they have no root, they last only a short time. When trouble or persecution comes because of the word, they quickly fall away. Still others, like seed sown among thorns, hear the word; but the worries of this life, the deceitfulness of wealth and the desires for other things come in and choke the word, making it unfruitful. Others, like seed sown on good soil, hear the word, accept it, and produce a crop – some thirty, some sixty, some a hundred times what was sown." **(Mark 4:15-20)**

MESSAGE

Jesus seemed skeptical of large crowds. If you're trying to appease the masses, after all, you don't usually start your sales pitch with hating your father and mother or carrying your own torture device (Luke 14:25-27). But that's because Jesus wasn't summoning everyone to be half-hearted believers in him. He was summoning the people who would call him "Lord" and then *respond* like they meant it. He was looking for the radicals. "Radical" would probably translate to something like "crazy" in today's culture. Most people take the broad road. Most people, intentionally or not, fail to become "good soil" – they may hear God's word, and they may even accept it, but they do not *produce*. As Francis Chan says in "Crazy Love," we aren't called to "lukewarm Christianity," this idea that we can be as minimally godly as can be and still claim Jesus. We are called to be *obsessed* with Jesus. To listen to his word and then *do what it says* (James 1:22-25). Just like everyone has the option to be healthier by skipping fast food, everyone has the option to find true life by walking Jesus' narrow path. It takes a radical reality, centered on him.

RESPONSE

Truly walking with Jesus often looks a lot more uncomfortable, unorthodox and compassionate than we expect. How can you be more radical for him? **Hear his word** and pray for a renewed heart to **respond**.

81

"Spiritual maturity doesn't come by a strong will but a surrendered life."

David Welker

breathe

· pause · take a deep breath · recognize that God is here

SCRIPTURE

Then (Jesus) said to them all: "Whoever wants to be my disciple must deny themselves and take up their cross daily and follow me." **(Luke 9:23)** … "I am the gate; whoever enters through me will be saved. They will come in and go out, and find pasture. The thief comes only to steal and kill and destroy; I have come that they may have life, and have it to the full. I am the good shepherd. The good shepherd lays down his life for the sheep … I am the good shepherd; I know my sheep and my sheep know me – just as the Father knows me and I know the Father – and I lay down my life for the sheep." **(John 10:9-11, 14-15)**

MESSAGE

Only a few days into parenthood, a few of our friends brought us dinner. It was a touching gesture, especially with me, my wife and our new son fresh out of the hospital. But I'll never forget the feeling I had that night. It came from the pit of my stomach. It was a sense of *loss*. I was so happy to see our friends, and very excited to be a dad, but there was also this heavy realization that nothing would ever be the way it used to be. My time was no longer just *my* time. I lost the freedom to spend hours on end with those friends, or eat that dinner without a care in the world. And yet, as time went on and I grew to know our baby, the source of that scary feeling, things reverted closer and closer to normalcy – except with the added joy of a little guy by my side. I can't help but see this as a picture of our relationship with Jesus. We hear about "taking up our cross" all the time, but as pastor David Welker says, carrying your "cross" doesn't mean encountering difficulties in life. Instead, "the cross is the place where you and I get crossed out." It's where we *die* along with Jesus – our ego, our demands, our rights. And much like my son's presence went from a bitter loss of self to an unparalleled gain of joy, our "crucifixion" with Jesus isn't ultimately a promise of misery. As Christians, we *do* suffer loss – we lose ourselves. But in doing so, we *gain* life (Matthew 16:25). We are *sheep*, not wolves, because we *have* the Good Shepherd, leading us to the best pastures.

RESPONSE

Jesus came so that you may have life "to the full." He is our reason for hope, joy and peace both here, on Earth, and for eternity to come. Think about what he offers – and asks, in return. Are *you* crossed out for his glory? Are you allowing him to be your shepherd?

breathe

· pause   · take a deep breath   · recognize that God is here

SCRIPTURE ⌐⌐

"Those of you who do not give up everything you have cannot be my disciples." **(Luke 14:33)** ... Jesus answered, "If you want to be perfect, go, sell your possessions and give to the poor, and you will have treasure in heaven. Then come, follow me." When the young man heard this, he went away sad, because he had great wealth. Then Jesus said to his disciples, "Truly I tell you, it is hard for someone who is rich to enter the kingdom of heaven. Again I tell you, it is easier for a camel to go through the eye of a needle than for someone who is rich to enter the kingdom of God." **(Matthew 19:21-23)**

MESSAGE 💬

There are plenty of people whose idea of Christianity starts and ends with showing up for Sunday morning coffee, or attending the yearly Easter service. But you don't have to look hard in the Bible to realize that following Jesus was – and is supposed to be – uncomfortable. How else do you describe giving up *everything*? How else do you explain Jesus telling potential disciples that he is all but homeless? That they should forget about burying their own fathers in order to go with him (Matthew 8:18-22)? That they should sell *everything* they own! Now, I can't say for sure that God actually wants us to give away our cars and go live on the street, but I think our relationship with comfort can be an indicator of our relationship with God. Imagine if Jesus asked us to give up our Wi-Fi. How many of us would say, "You can have anything but that!" There is good to be found in comfort, but too much of it can lead us astray. When we reach a point where our comforts (from air-conditioned homes to on-demand entertainment to our own schedules) become more necessary than Jesus and his mission, it's probably time for a wakeup call. Consider these words from the song "Uncomfortable," by Andy Mineo: *Nobody told me you could die from bliss ... If you want to live a comfortable life, make sure you never love nobody, be selfish and never sacrifice.*

RESPONSE 🙏

Comfort is attractive. It allow us to escape our vulnerabilities. But as Jesus followers, we know that it's not an ultimate means of satisfaction on this side of eternity. Which comforts do you cling to? How has being comfortable or uncomfortable shaped your relationship with God? Try **leaving your comfort zone** in a specific way this week.

breathe

· pause   · take a deep breath   · recognize that God is here

• our only fear and deepest love •

SCRIPTURE

I have a message from God in my heart concerning the sinfulness of the wicked: There is no fear of God before their eyes. **(Psalm 36:1)** ... The fear of the Lord is the beginning of wisdom. **(Proverbs 9:10)** ... But the eyes of the Lord are on those who fear him, on those whose hope is in his unfailing love. **(Psalm 33:18)** ... Blessed are all who fear the Lord, who walk in obedience to him. **(Psalm 128:1)** ... The fear of the Lord is a fountain of life, turning a person from the snares of death. **(Proverbs 14:27)**

MESSAGE

Francis Chan suggests a simple question can help determine if you're on fire for Jesus: Is God your *only* fear and your *deepest* love? Fear and love are two different things, but they can work hand in hand. Anyone who's ever had a mom or dad can attest to this, because it's very possible to love your parents and also be afraid of them. If you do something you're not supposed to, you fear their consequences. And just like good parents will use consequences for their kids' benefit, the Bible's urges to "fear the Lord" are linked with *good* things: Wisdom, blessing, a fountain of life. It's no surprise, then, that one of the chief signs of wickedness, as Psalm 36:1 says, is having *no* fear of God. Think about it: How are we to fully grasp Jesus' grace and mercy if we aren't also fearful of his justice and power? He is our one true love *because* he is our one true fear. We're told that God disciplines the ones He loves (Hebrews 12:6), and Jesus, despite coming as a ransom for all, insists that he *will* punish the unrighteous (Matthew 10:28). If you don't think God punishes, just try reading Genesis 6 or Exodus 12 or Jesus' many teachings on Hell. We have a parental picture here: We know Jesus loves us and wants the best for us, and we fear him out of respect for that. In "The Pleasures of God," John Piper puts it like so: "The fear of God is what is left of the storm when you have a safe place to watch right in the middle of it ... the thrill of being ... in the center of the awful power of God, yet protected by God himself!"

RESPONSE

We fear many things, and we love many things. Just know that Jesus desires to be feared and loved the *most*. God is a good father, and He doesn't ask for mindless compliance. He asks for *us*, as children. He wants us to know His power but also know His love. **Rest** in this beauty, that God is our willing refuge from His own storms! He will bring about justice, but He has gifted us Jesus, who intercedes for us (Romans 8:34).

breathe

• pause   • take a deep breath   • recognize that God is here

SCRIPTURE 📖

Now faith is confidence in what we hope for and assurance about what we do not see ... And without faith it is impossible to please God, because anyone who comes to him must believe that he exists and that he rewards those who earnestly seek him. **(Hebrews 11:1, 6)** ... For we live by faith, not by sight. **(2 Corinthians 5:7)** ... May the God of hope fill you with all joy and peace as you trust in him, so that you may overflow with hope by the power of the Holy Spirit. **(Romans 15:13)**

MESSAGE 💬

"Let go and let God." If you've been around Christianity long enough, you've probably heard this phrase before, even if it's been reduced to text on glossy, inspirational social media posts (#Blessed!). It has a little bit of truth, perhaps, for certain occasions. But I think I prefer this one, from former C.S. Lewis student J.I. Packer: "Trust God and get going." There's an *action* there. A *movement* in belief. An *embodying* of His Kingdom and presence. God will be God, yes, but to "live by faith" is to *live*, not just wait around. I couldn't have married my wife without choosing *trust* rather than the uncertainties of the future. I wouldn't have *met* my wife if I hadn't chosen trust over the comfort of staying at home from a summer-long trip to inner-city Detroit. Both of those decisions, of course, weren't "blind" leaps. They were backed by prayer, by other believers, by the Spirit's tug. But they were fulfilled in action, by *stepping out*. We see time and time again God rewarding those who put their faith in action (Abraham, Noah, Moses, Rahab are all referenced in Hebrews 11), so we shouldn't be afraid to trust Him and "get going." As Dr. Martin Luther King Jr. says, "Faith is taking the first step even when you don't see the whole staircase."

RESPONSE 🙏

When the Bible nudges us to walk in faith, it doesn't mean to be careless, but it *can* mean to be bold and maybe a little uncomfortable. The best part: God rewards faith! You bear fruit, advance His Kingdom and get more of *Him*! Stepping out in faith doesn't always have to be a major decision, either, like moving across the country. It can be as simple as saying "no" to your busy schedule and taking a moment with God. Or complimenting someone despite it being "awkward." Or talking to the stranger you'd normally look past. **Take a step**, and see what the Lord does.

breathe

· pause   · take a deep breath   · recognize that God is here

SCRIPTURE

I denied myself nothing my eyes desired; I refused my heart no pleasure ... Yet when I surveyed all that my hands had done and what I had toiled to achieve, everything was meaningless, a chasing after the wind ... The wise have eyes in their heads, while the fool walks in the darkness; but I came to realize that the same fate overtakes them both. **(Ecclesiastes 2:10-11, 14)** ... Whoever loves money never has enough; whoever loves wealth is never satisfied with their income. **(5:10)** ... Everyone comes naked from their mother's womb, and as everyone comes, so they depart. **(5:15)** ... This is the evil in everything that happens under the sun: The same destiny overtakes all. The hearts of people ... there is madness in their hearts while they live, and afterward they join the dead. **(9:3)**

MESSAGE

Ecclesiastes isn't the most cheery book in the Bible, but I absolutely love it, probably because it speaks so much into a problem that haunts humanity to this day. As a culture, we may trivialize or just flat-out ignore the harsh reality that everyone dies, that "no one remembers" past generations (1:11), that literally *everything* on this Earth is fleeting. But that doesn't make it any less true. You can give your heart every pleasure you can possibly find, and death still awaits. Reputations are forged, then forgotten. Treasures never satisfy. It's the story of our lives! And you'd think that one celebrity suicide after another would help us realize it. If the most successful people in the world (by the world's standards) ultimately find that life isn't worth living, why do we keep following the same script, chasing the same things – fame, wealth, power, wisdom – as if they'll *finally* come through for us? The entire book is a cold dose of reality, reminding us that everything is meaningless if our hope lies no further than mankind. Do you see how this points to Jesus? When we see the darkness of the world, the light of Christ becomes all the more bright. We see our need for refuge, and we find it in him! His sweet peace contrasts the toils of life.

RESPONSE

On one hand, it can be sobering to know that everything truly is temporary in this world. On another hand, it should be awesome to know that Jesus, our loving God, is with us always. Unlike the momentary pleasures that attract, then disappoint us, he offers true, unending rest. **Read** Ecclesiastes, then look to Jesus' warmth!

breathe

· pause · take a deep breath · recognize that God is here

SCRIPTURE

For our present troubles are small and won't last very long. Yet they produce for us a glory that vastly outweighs them and will last forever! **(2 Corinthians 4:17)** ... For we know that when this earthly tent we live in is taken down (that is, when we die and leave this earthly body), we will have a house in heaven, an eternal body made for us by God himself and not by human hands. **(2 Corinthians 5:1)** ... "My Father's house has many rooms; if that were not so, would I have told you that I am going there to prepare a place for you? And if I go and prepare a place for you, I will come back and take you to be with me that you also may be where I am." **(John 14:2-3)**

MESSAGE

When I was younger, I imagined Heaven as this bland space in the clouds, overcrowded with people. There'd be times I would imagine being there forever and start to feel *scared*. Like, won't it get old? As Randy Alcorn writes in "Heaven," the Devil probably smiled at that thinking. He *wants* us to be bored with Heaven. But the Bible paints a different picture. We're told to *look forward to* our future dwelling place (2 Peter 3:13). We're promised resurrected *bodies*, much like that of Jesus, who has flesh and bones, hunger and thirst – physical things (Luke 24:36-43). And we're bound for an actual place, a New Earth with cities, rivers, streets (Revelation 21-22). An old friend once told me that if we didn't see each other again, I could look for him in the mountains in Heaven. I love that image. It gets me *excited* for eternity, which "creation itself" awaits (Romans 8:18-25)! And that's not even mentioning the best part: Jesus. Heaven has its perks, from the endless friendships to the new creation. But as John Piper notes, Heaven without Jesus would be Hell. (It's why C.S. Lewis suggests those in Hell ultimately choose to be there, getting the "horrible freedom" from God they demand.) Because what's greater than the physical presence of Jesus, the one who loves us like no other? What could be better than knowing and living with our very Creator?

RESPONSE

If Jesus is just your ticket to Heaven, you'll miss out on the here and now. But living *in light of* Heaven is also key. It puts suffering in perspective. It inspires us to live for what lasts. And it gives us true, ultimate hope. **Look forward** to being with Jesus! To die is gain. Though his presence is with us now, *he* awaits us in glory!

95

breathe

· pause   · take a deep breath   · recognize that God is here

• like little children •

SCRIPTURE

At that time the disciples came to Jesus and asked, "Who, then, is the greatest in the kingdom of heaven?" He called a little child to him, and placed the child among them. And he said: "Truly I tell you, unless you change and become like little children, you will never enter the kingdom of heaven. Therefore, whoever takes the lowly position of this child is the greatest in the kingdom of heaven." **(Matthew 18:1-4)** ... "Truly I tell you, anyone who will not receive the kingdom of God like a little child will never enter it." **(Luke 18:17)** ... "For those who exalt themselves will be humbled, and those who humble themselves will be exalted." **(Matthew 23:12)**

MESSAGE

How odd this must have been for Jesus' disciples at the time. Here was God in the flesh, with a direct opportunity to explain who is most highly regarded in his kingdom. And who does he grab? A kid. In doing so, I don't think Jesus intended for his disciples to become *childish* (Paul tells us in 1 Corinthians 14:20 not to be children in our thinking) but rather to be *childlike* in our reception of him. He explains in Matthew: "Whoever takes the *lowly* position of this child" is doing it right. Not only are kids literally in a lowly position in regards to adults, but they are marked with meekness, dependence and openness. Have you ever noticed how (painfully) observant children can be? How they aren't afraid to speak their minds, or ask questions? And how, at a young age, they rely fully on others? At age 30, we might be wrapped up in our own ambitions, convinced of our self-sufficiency, living without constant neediness. At age 3, however, we're pretty weak. We're small. We're needy. It's *that* kind of approach that not only brings us closer to Jesus but models his very life (Matthew 23:11). Those of us who put Jesus *before* ourselves will inherit his kingdom and carry his presence. Those who are *last* will be *first* (Matthew 19:30).

RESPONSE

Has it hit you how unusual this probably sounds to the rest of the world? We tend to think that *more* is better – more power, more independence, more whatever. Jesus tells us that *less* is more when it comes to connecting with him. Less of us, more of him. **Know** God desires your observations, your questions, your childlike dependence. Know He is glorified in your weakness (2 Corinthians 12:9). Know you are His beloved child. **Receive** Him.

breathe

· pause · take a deep breath · recognize that God is here

SCRIPTURE

I do not understand what I do. For what I want to do I do not do, but what I hate I do … For I have the desire to do what is good, but I cannot carry it out … So I find this law at work: Although I want to do good, evil is right there with me. For in my inner being I delight in God's law; but I see another law at work in me, waging war against the law of my mind and making me a prisoner of the law of sin at work within me. What a wretched man I am! Who will rescue me from this body that is subject to death? Thanks be to God, who delivers me through Jesus Christ our Lord! **(Romans 7:14-15, 18, 21-25)**

MESSAGE

Two of the biggest struggles I've had in my relationship with God are 1.) giving God the time He deserves and 2.) seeing Him for who He is. To the first point, why on Earth has it sometimes been so easy for me to claim Christ, spend time with his followers and discuss "spiritual stuff," yet fail to fully enjoy *him*? How can I know, in my mind, that Jesus provides true life, but then never pause *my* life to receive it? Am I unconvinced that starting or ending my day with God will make that much of a difference? Am I taking life for granted, valuing gifts more than the Giver? Am I too comfortable, to the point where only a slow buildup of problems will send me to His arms? To the second point, on the rare occasion I *do* take a moment with God, why is that so often I'm just there to ask Him for something? Why am I not choosing Jesus for *Jesus*, and not just for *me*? I'm not sure there are clear-cut answers to any of these questions, but I think they're worth wrestling with, and I pray they spark some of your own. At our core, all of us are incapable of fully living the way we know we should. But as Paul says in Romans 7, thank God for God! Because of Jesus, He smiles at us anyway.

RESPONSE

If you're like me and desire to know Jesus better, first **ask** God for a *hunger* for Him, for a revelation of how much you *need* Him. Then **practice** engaging Him. Start small, if you must. Jesus beckons us to a quiet place (Mark 6:31). Go there. Close your eyes. Just pray one thing. Or read just a few verses and sit with them. Or write one prayer. Or just sit in silence and listen. Be with Him, and see where He takes you.

"Yes, I'm a Christian. Yes, I make hypocritical decisions. Yes, I fall. I stumble. I am a mess. But I'm God's mess. And he can turn a mess into a masterpiece."

Lecrae

breathe

· pause   · take a deep breath   · recognize that God is here

SCRIPTURE

" ... Christ loved the church and gave himself up for her." **(Ephesians 5:25)** ... Like the rest, we were by nature deserving of wrath. But because of his great love for us, God, who is rich in mercy, made us alive with Christ even when we were dead in transgressions – it is by grace you have been saved. **(Ephesians 2:3-5)** ... Blessed is the one whose transgressions are forgiven, whose sins are covered. Blessed is the one whose sin the Lord does not count against them ... I acknowledged my sin to you and did not cover up my iniquity. I said, "I will confess my transgressions to the Lord." And you forgave the guilt of my sin. **(Psalm 32:1-2, 5)** ... Jesus said to them, "It is not the healthy who need a doctor, but the sick. I have not come to call the righteous, but sinners." **(Mark 2:17)**

MESSAGE

So often when I hear John 3:16 – or any teaching about Jesus redeeming people from sin, for that matter – I acknowledge that Christ has come to save us without putting myself in the "us." I forget to remind myself that "our sins" are also *my* sins. That Jesus Christ came and lived and died with *me* in mind. That it's *my* sin, not sin in general, that separated me from God. That Jesus "loving the church" doesn't mean him loving an institution, or a people *group*, but loving people like you and me. That Jesus went to the cross knowing, in his divine heart, "Cody is going to be born on April 9, 1994, in Lancaster, Pennsylvania, and he's going to need my grace." Doesn't that stir you? There is *power* in our weakness, in admitting that we can't clean ourselves up except by looking to the cross and seeing God suffer for our personal sickness. C.S. Lewis says that those "who do not think about their own sins make up for it by thinking incessantly about the sins of others." I'd argue those people (and I've been one!) also make up for it by pretending how righteous they are apart from Christ. It's no wonder Paul takes *delight* (!) in weaknesses and hardships, for they point him back to the One who saves (2 Corinthians 12:10).

RESPONSE

Re-read the Scripture section, except with your name in place of "the church" and other plurals. Make your weakness *personal*, and let Jesus become *your* hope, not just a broad idea or symbol. **See** and confront your own sins (1 John 1:8-10). And find strength and peace knowing Jesus is for *you*. Carry your thanks with you.

103

"Human beings do not readily admit desperation.
When they do, the kingdom of heaven draws near."

Philip Yancey

breathe

• pause   • take a deep breath   • recognize that God is here

• the only well of life •

SCRIPTURE 📖

"Jesus is 'the stone you builders rejected, which has become the cornerstone.' Salvation is found in no one else, for there is no other name under heaven given to mankind by which we must be saved." **(Acts 4:11-12)** … Whoever believes in him is not condemned, but whoever does not believe stands condemned already because they have not believed in the name of God's one and only Son. This is the verdict: Light has come into the world, but people loved darkness instead of light because their deeds were evil. **(John 3:18-19)** … And so I tell you, every kind of sin and slander can be forgiven, but blasphemy against the Spirit will not be forgiven. **(Matthew 12:31)**

MESSAGE 💬

Jesus' warning in Matthew 12:31 that "blasphemy against the Spirit will not be forgiven" can be confounding. But as Josh Porter, of Bridgetown Church, says, the easiest way to explain it is this: If you're concerned you may have committed the sin, you haven't. Blasphemy against the spirit is not "careless acts," but rather an "unwillingness to repent." That also explains why it won't be forgiven. "It's not just that you won't be forgiven," Porter says. "It's that you can't be … Once you declare that the only remaining bottle of water is poison, you condemn yourself to dying of thirst." C.S. Lewis echoes this, "Does it matter to a man dying in a desert by which choice of route he missed the only well?" In other words, the *only* thing that will destroy us is a failure to believe in the One who saves us. See how Jesus prefaces this by saying *every kind* of sin can be forgiven. He *starts* with the wideness of his mercy and forgiveness! His caution is simply not to reject that same mercy and forgiveness, or the need for it. God's mission, Porter says, is to end evil, rescue its victims and redeem its abusers. But He will not force anyone. "Some who do evil would rather not be rescued, let alone redeemed," Porter concludes. "Yet He is still coming."

RESPONSE 🙏

How marvelous Jesus' promises are for those who simply put their trust in him. When we realize that *no* sin can separate us from his love, we are free to rejoice in our freedom and long for his return. Whoever believes in him, who trusts in him, is *not condemned*. Repent, knowing that Jesus cleanses you. And **reflect** on his promise to rescue and redeem the unjust people (that's you and me!) who simply accept his gift.

"Your propensity to trash your life is no match for God's ability to recycle it."

John Onwuchekwa

breathe

· pause · take a deep breath · recognize that God is here

SCRIPTURE

I have been crucified with Christ and I no longer live, but Christ lives in me. **(Galatians 2:20)** … I urge you … in view of God's mercy, to offer your bodies as a living sacrifice, holy and pleasing to God – this is your true and proper worship. Do not conform to the pattern of this world, but be transformed by the renewing of your mind. Then you will be able to test and approve what God's will is – his good, pleasing and perfect will. **(Romans 12:1-2)** … So whether you eat or drink or whatever you do, do it all for the glory of God. **(1 Corinthians 10:31)**

MESSAGE

The "golden mean" is a term from ancient Greek philosophy used to describe the "desirable middle" between two extremes. In essence, it is perfect *balance*. Many times, in pondering faith-related questions, I've found the "right answer" to be exactly that – to strike a balance, or find the "desirable middle." After all, too *much* or too *little* of anything – church responsibilities, family, friends, downtime, politics, entertainment, you name it – is unhealthy. Think about your relationship with Jesus: It's not fueled *only* by the Word, or *only* by the Spirit, or *only* by other believers, but through a *balance* of them all. What I've found, however, is that the most effective way to live in that healthy medium is not to rely more on my own *dos* and *don'ts*, but rather give *everything* over to Jesus. To let him completely renew my heart. To let God's *character* inform *whatever* I do. To a *new creation* rather than an old one that tries harder. To be *remade*, as C.S. Lewis writes:

"Christ says, 'Give me all. I don't want just this much of your time and this much of your money and this much of your work … I will give you a new self instead. Hand over the whole natural self – all the desires, not just the ones you think wicked but the ones you think innocent – the whole outfit … The almost impossibly hard thing is to hand over your whole self to Christ. But it is far easier than what we are all trying to do instead. For what we are trying to do is remain what we call 'ourselves' – our personal happiness centered on money or pleasure or ambition – and hoping, despite this, to behave honestly and chastely and humbly … (We) must be plowed up and re-sown."

RESPONSE

Where do you need more balance? **Invite** Jesus into this area. Allow him to totally renew and guide you.

notes

To further explore ideas and quotes used in **Hi, God**, we highly recommend the following sources, which were used and cited, both directly and indirectly, throughout the devotional:

- C.S. Lewis, *Mere Christianity*, Geoffrey Bles, 1952
  - **Lewis is always a must-read, but particularly here, where he makes the case for Jesus Christ as common, intellectual sense**
- Tony Reinke, *12 Ways Your Phone is Changing You*, Crossway, 2017
  - **Thoughtful commentary on how the digital age's most accessible device, the smartphone, affects our relationship with Jesus, the Church, its people and our lives, in general**
- Tony Reinke, "Compressing Spiritual Growth in the Age of Acceleration," TonyReinke.com, March 2019
- John Gill, *Gill's Exposition of the Entire Bible*, BibleHub.com/commentaries/gill
- Bob Goff, *Everybody, Always*, Nelson Books, 2018
  - **Simple but delightful, this is like a How-To on living with an abundance of love**
- C.S. Lewis, *How to Pray*, HarperOne, 2018
- Alan Noble, *Disruptive Witness*, InterVarsity Press, 2018
- *The New City Catechism*, Crossway, The Gospel Coalition, NewCityCatechism.com, 2017-2019
  - **A Q&A-style resource that pairs Scripture with both old and new commentaries, from Martin Luther to Tim Keller, to explore 52 core principles of faith; available as an interactive app**
- Matt Chandler, "That Which Satisfies," The Village Church, 2019, TVCResources.net
- Matt Chandler, "That You May Marvel," The Village Church, 2019, TVCResources.net
- Francis Chan, *Crazy Love*, David C Cook, 2008
  - **An absolute must-read example of what it looks like to be *in love* with Jesus**
- John Mark Comer, "God Has A Name | Yahweh," Bridgetown Church, 2013, Bridgetown.Church
- A.J. Swoboda, "Subversive Sabbath," Bridgetown Church, 2019, Bridgetown.Church
- R.C. Sproul, *Saved from What?*, Crossway, 2002

- Trevin Wax, *This Is Our Time: Everyday Myths in Light of the Gospel*, B&H Books, 2017
  - **Very topical and engaging look at age-old issues in a modern setting, from the idolization of money and politics, to the distortion of marriage, to the pursuit of happiness**
- Josh Porter, "Gospel of Matthew: Brood of Vipers," Bridgetown Church, 2019, Bridgetown.Church
- David Welker, "Advent Revelation, Jesus the Lion and the Lamb," Two Rivers Vineyard Church, 2018, TRVC.org/sermons
- John Piper, *The Pleasures of God*, Multnomah, 2000
- Andy Mineo, "Uncomfortable," *Uncomfortable*, Reach Records, 2015
- Philip Yancey, *The Jesus I Never Knew*, Zondervan, 1995
- "Chris Pratt's 9 Rules Acceptance Speech | 2018 MTV Movie & TV Awards," MTV, YouTube, 2018
- Francis Chan, "The Cost of Discipleship," YouTube, 2015
- C.S. Lewis, *The Great Divorce*, Geoffrey Bles, 1945
  - **Fascinating allegory about Heaven and Hell, good and evil**

about the author

Cody Benjamin is an author and journalist based in Southern Minnesota.

Originally from Pennsylvania, Cody currently writes for CBS Sports and serves as a pastoral intern for Two Rivers Vineyard Church in Mankato, where he lives with his wife, Brooke, and their son, Emmanuel. He previously served as a youth ministry coordinator in Blue Earth, Minnesota, and has written for SB Nation, LNP News (Lancaster Newspapers) and the Faribault County (Minn.) Register.

A graduate of Indiana University of Pennsylvania, Cody has written five other books, all of which are available online via Lulu.com, Amazon, GoodReads and Barnes & Noble:

Hatched | an unofficially definitive guide to the 2017 Super Bowl champion Philadelphia Eagles
Cabin | a collection of Christian devotionals
The Eagles Notebook | reflections on a life influenced by Eagles fandom and coverage
Outcast | a commentary on Christianity in contemporary culture
Skyline Teardrops | a diary from a summer spent volunteering in inner-city Detroit

Outside of writing and the occasional guest sermon, Cody can usually be found at a movie theater, watching Philly sports, ensuring that his son likes Philly sports, or eating pasta.

@CodyJBenjamin | CodyJBenjamin@gmail.com